Background	Pupils gain an understanding of the historical, political and religious context in which Jesus lived. They develop an awareness of how various practices and ways of life in New Testament times stem from religious beliefs and teachings.
Visualisation	The use of creative visualisation helps develop pupils' imagination, curiosity and insight.
Reflection	Prompts for reflection develop pupils' capacity to respond to questions of meaning and purpose, and to reflect on their own values, beliefs and sources of inspiration.
Discussion	By sharing their views and listening to others, pupils develop self-awareness and open-mindedness.

What is guided visualisation?

Visualisation involves using the power of the imagination to recall the shape and size of an object, or a situation. Visualisations are most "real" when other senses besides the visual are employed, such as smells, sounds, tastes, textures and how something feels to the touch, associated with a known experience. Guided visualisation is when the pupil is led through a story sequence. The visualisation is narrated in the second person present tense, giving the pupil an active part in the story, often in the role of a bystander. It is sometimes referred to as creative visualisation, guided imagery, or guided fantasy. We prefer to use the term "guided visualisation" because it is an accurate, unambiguous description.

Why use guided visualisation in RE?

Guided visualisation has particular value in RE because it engages pupils in a personal way and helps develop their ability for reflection. Moreover, it is inclusive in that the learning process does not involve reading or writing, and pupils who generally struggle in this respect are not disadvantaged. At the same time it allows scope for differentiation in that the visualisations can be accessed at different levels, and pupils can be extended through the discussion and follow up activities. A further reason for using guided visualisation in RE is that children enjoy it, and this helps them enter into learning wholeheartedly.

Historical visualisations

Most of the visualisations are historical in the sense that pupils are led through a story sequence set within an historical context. Here imagery and commentary can help pupils understand the socio-political world in which Jesus lived. As pupils observe what happens they are simultaneously engaged in a process of interpretation as they try to make sense of the main issues and themes.

There are different ways of using historical visualisation. One is where the entire story is told within the visualisation. This means that although pupils have been given background information, they do not necessarily have prior knowledge of the story. During the visualisation they are hearing it for the first time. Another way is to give some of the story beforehand. In 'The Arrest' for example, the first part of the story is read from the New Testament. Then, at a key point, the story is suspended. Anticipation raises interest, and the pupils are keen to know what happens next. They are then invited to enter into the story via visualisation to observe the remaining dramatic events as they unfold.

Thematic visualisations

Where the main learning outcome is to explore a theme, it is not always necessary for the visualisation to be set in New Testament times. It may be appropriate to examine a theme outside the biblical context if this assists pupils to learn in a way that is engaging, accessible and meaningful to them. The setting may be contemporary, or remind them of a popular book or film. For example, in the lesson entitled 'The Lost Coin', pupils are led to the Chamber of Safekeeping to think about things that are valuable to themselves and others.

Questions for reflection and discussion

Reflection and discussion is an essential part of the lesson. It is the point at which pupils are challenged to think more deeply, and the teacher can assess more precisely what learning has taken place. Discussion can be in groups or whole class. If pupils are given a few moments to think through their own response first, before sharing with a partner or group, there is more opportunity for developing personal reflection, which is a key component of AT2 learning. This can be followed up with an invitation to some kind of written or visually creative response allowing further opportunity for assessment.

What about the answers?

There is never one right answer to any of the really important questions in life. Pupils show that they are learning from religion not by knowing the right answers but by learning to raise and reflect on the right kind of questions. In the non-statutory national framework for RE the level 4 descriptor for Attainment Target 2 says:

> Pupils raise, and suggest answers to, questions of identity, belonging, meaning, purpose, truth, values and commitments. They apply their ideas to their own and other people's lives. They describe what inspires and influences themselves and others.[3]

The main concern would appear to be in developing pupils' ability to engage with the questioning process, and this approach certainly does that! If pupils are able to raise questions, and suggest answers of their own they are really getting to grips with some of the issues as well as meeting the requirement of AT2 learning. This is why, directly following a story, the pupils are asked if they have any questions or comments. This provides an opportunity to clear up any misunderstandings, as well as showing pupils that their questions are important.

---

3 Religious Education: The non-statutory national framework: *Attainment targets for Religious Education*, p.36, (QCA, 2004).

"See" RE

Stories from Christianity

Mary Stone and **Jill Brennan**

RMEP

Religious and Moral Education Press
Editorial office: 13–17 Long Lane, London EC1A 9PN
www.rmep.co.uk
RMEP is an imprint of Hymns Ancient & Modern Ltd (a registered charity), St Mary's Works, St Mary's Plain, Norwich, Norfolk NR3 3BH, UK

First published 2009

A catalogue record for this book is available from the British Library

ISBN 987-1-85175-455-7

Acknowledgements
We would like to thank the following people:
Sue Holmes, for getting the ball rolling
Jackie Wright for another teacher's eye over the manuscript
Children of High Bank First and Copley Primary School.

Bible extracts quoted from the *Good News Bible* published by The Bible Societies/ HarperCollins Publishers Ltd, UK, © American Bible Society, 1966, 1971, 1976, 1992.

To find out more about visualisations, go to www.see-re.co.uk

Designed and typeset by Regent Typesetting, London
Cover design by TOPICS – The Creative Partnership, Exeter

Printed in Great Britain by Information Press, Eynsham, Oxford, OX29 4JB

Contents

Introduction

"See" RE is a collection of lesson plans for use in primary schools with pupils aged between 7 and 11. Written by teachers for teachers, it is intended to be a user-friendly resource both to supplement planning, and as a prompt in the classroom.

"See" refers to the use of guided visualisation to facilitate learning. "RE" relates to the subject content, here based on stories found in the New Testament. Some are stories Jesus told, and others are narratives about the life of Jesus. The material is non-confessional, and is suitable for use in all primary schools.

At present Religious Education is taught according to a locally agreed syllabus.[1] Though as yet there is no national programme of study for Religious Education, there has been a move in that direction with the publication of the non-statutory national framework.[2] It is this non-statutory national framework that informs most Agreed Syllabuses, as many have been revised in accordance with these guidelines. This may also apply to diocesan syllabuses but to a lesser extent. Therefore, whilst in the introduction to each lesson, possible learning outcomes are suggested, you are advised to check that these are compliant with your locally agreed syllabus when planning to use this material.

The material is organised as lesson plans. Each story, and its associated activities, is designed as one RE lesson for which we suggest an allocated time of 45 minutes minimum. An indication of the QCA level that could be reached within the lesson is given at the top of the page beside the title.

The QCA non-statutory national framework states that there are two aspects to pupils' learning in Religious Education: learning about religion (AT1) and learning from religion (AT2). Achieving a balance of coverage within a single lesson can present something of a challenge, especially with regard to those elusive AT2 objectives! The lesson plans have been compiled with this in mind, and aim to balance both aspects of attainment target requirement. Assessment is so much easier if learning outcomes and appropriate activities have been thought through.

The different components of the lesson support the non-statutory national framework for Religious Education in the following ways:

Story	Through the stories pupils become familiar with the life and teachings of Jesus, and know that these stories are found in the New Testament. The stories can be re-told in the teacher's own words, perhaps dramatised using children to represent the key characters. Alternatively, pupils could be asked to find the stories themselves from a given biblical reference if copies of the New Testament are available. This helps to reinforce learning that the New Testament is the primary source of the stories.
Vocabulary	Attention is drawn to any vocabulary or religious terminology that may need to be explained. Pupils are encouraged to use religious language to demonstrate their knowledge and understanding.

---

1 This is the case for all maintained schools – voluntary-aided religious schools being the exception.
2 Religious Education: The non-statutory national framework (QCA, London 2004).

However if, as is likely, a child asks you what the answer is, caution is advised. Any response you give will undoubtedly reflect either just one interpretation within a very broad "Christian" spectrum, or a secularist bias, which some would argue is just another form of indoctrination. If you must provide an answer, be sure to pre-text with the words, "some people believe" or "some Christians believe". You could offer to tell the class your own thoughts on the matter at the end of the lesson. This helps keep the lesson focused on the children's ideas and thought processes, and at the same time it raises curiosity. Pupils will realise that you as an individual are entitled to an opinion, just as they are. Furthermore what you say may differ from what another teacher says. Rather than being problematic this helps pupils begin to understand that with regard to religious understanding, truth is always subjective.

How to "do" guided visualisation

Firstly, in order to create the right conditions, try to ensure that the room you are using is reasonably quiet, and you are unlikely to be disturbed. Arrange the chairs so the children are facing you. (If they face one another across a table, they are likely to become self-conscious and check to see what others are doing, or indeed if anyone is watching them!) Then ask the children to sit comfortably … relax their shoulders … gently close their eyes … and become aware of their own breathing. Try to use the same words each time when you lead into and come out of a visualisation. This will then become a kind of ritual, helping the children know what's going to happen next, and what is expected of them. Beginnings and endings are included in the visualisation script, but a few alternatives are suggested below, and you can always customise your own. The phrase "sit alert and relaxed" can be used with children as young as Reception age, if the language is explained as follows: "When I say alert I mean being wide awake, and relaxed means being comfortable."

When reading the visualisation narrative, finding the right pace is very important. Slowing down your voice, and pausing between phrases will help to create an atmosphere of stillness and calm, and give pupils the thinking time they need within the exercise. The use of ellipsis indicates where a pause should be slightly longer. Achieve the right pace of delivery by checking with the children afterwards: was it too fast, or too slow? It may be advisable to try a stilling exercise before using the units to familiarise the children with the technique.[4] Teachers are sometimes hesitant to try this sort of thing *because* they think the children will find it strange, feel silly doing it, and perhaps play up. But it is surprising how quickly children adjust and cooperate precisely because it is something new, different and potentially interesting. You may even find it has its uses to help settle the class at other times, such as following a wet playtime!

---

4 Many schools have a copy of *Don't Just Do Something, Sit There* by Mary Stone (RMEP, 1995). See Section B, pp. 10–17 for notes on stilling, focussing attention and using all the senses.

Begin with	Sit in an alert and relaxed position …
	Place your hands gently on your knees.
	Close your eyes and be still.
	Become aware of your breathing.
End with	Now bring your mind back to the classroom.
	Become aware of the hardness of your chair.
	When you're ready wiggle your toes, open your eyes, and have a good stretch.

What if a child becomes emotional?

It isn't unusual for children to feel moved by the visualisations as they can be very powerful. On one occasion a visualisation with a Year 5 class focused on a close examination of the hands of Jesus. When it was over the pupils were asked to bring their minds back to the classroom and open their eyes. One boy kept his head down. Being a strong-willed character, it wasn't clear at first whether he was simply choosing not to conform. However, after a while the boy did lift his head, but not before wiping his eyes first with his sleeve. Situations such as this show that a child has engaged at a personal level, and taken something from the lesson that is meaningful and memorable to them. Of course, there is a difference between feeling moved by something, and becoming upset. If you anticipate that for personal reasons a particular child may become upset during the lesson, perhaps speak to them privately beforehand. Explain what the lesson will involve, and maybe give the option of time out at any point. In such cases we have generally found that children choose to be included. If they do become upset, they find the support they receive from other pupils helpful to them. The instinctive kindness children show to one another in such circumstances upholds a caring classroom ethos, and provides pupils the opportunity to express concern and consideration for others. This all goes towards helping develop empathy and emotional maturity.

What about the saboteurs!

We all know that some children find it easier to sit still than others. It may be necessary at first for a certain child or children to sit separately, away from the others but where you can see them. Explain that the reason for this is because their behaviour is distracting others, however, their chair is left empty and they can rejoin the class when they feel ready. When they see that the other children are getting into the visualisation, a combination of curiosity, peer pressure, boredom and not wanting to be left out may lead to their cooperation and unobtrusive joining in.

If you find anything else that works, use it!

Needless to say we are passionate about the use of guided visualisation in RE. Over the years we have used it to great effect in the classroom, and found the experience enjoyable and enriching.

Why not have a go and see for yourself!

Stories about Jesus

Temptation Level 4/5

Source: The New Testament: Luke 4:1–13 – the temptations in the wilderness.

AT1 Learning about religion: Pupils learn that Jesus faced temptation but remained true to his faith. They can explain how quoting scripture strengthened Jesus, helping him resist temptation.

AT2 Learning from religion: Pupils explore the meaning of temptation within a context they understand and suggest ways in which they might overcome this.

Vocabulary: worship, temptation, Holy Spirit, devil.

Background

1. Do the pupils understand what is meant by *temptation*? Ask for examples.
2. Ask the pupils to think about what is meant by "the devil". Is it a real person, or might it be something else? Does it have to be something you can see and hear? Could it be a thought inside your mind? Invite pupils to share their ideas.
3. Explain that the pupils will now look at, or hear a story from the New Testament about Jesus being tempted.

Ask the pupils to find the reference in the New Testament, read together or retell the story in your own words.

Jesus returned from the Jordan full of the Holy Spirit and was led by the Spirit into the desert, where he was tempted by the devil for 40 days. In all that time he ate nothing, so that he was hungry when it was over.

The devil said to him, "If you are God's son, order this stone to turn into bread."

But Jesus answered, "The scripture says; 'Human beings cannot live on bread alone.'"

Then the devil took him up and showed him in a second all the kingdoms of the world.

"I will give you all this power and all this wealth," the devil told him.

"It has been handed over to me, and I can give it to anyone I choose. All this will be yours then if you worship me."

Jesus answered, "The scripture says: 'Worship the Lord your God and serve only him!'"

Then the devil took him to Jerusalem and set him on the highest point of the Temple, and said to him, "If you are God's son, throw yourself down from here. For the scripture says: 'God will order his angels to take good care of you.' It also says: 'They will hold you up with their hands so that not even your feet will be hurt on the stones.'"

But Jesus answered, "The scripture says: 'Do not put the Lord your God to the test.'"

When the devil finished tempting Jesus in every way, he left him for a while.

Luke 4:1–13

- ➤ Are there any questions or comments?
- ➤ Why do you think the devil asks Jesus to turn the stones into bread?
- ➤ Do you think that quoting something helped him? How?

Visualisation

Sit alert and relaxed with your hands placed gently on your knees. Close your eyes and imagine …

… you watch as he sits in grubby clothes, on the rocky edge of the mountain …
Jesus is alone, or so it seems.
Until something disturbs him.

Notice how his face changes.
See, he leans forward to pick up a rock …
Turning it over slowly in his hands, he stares at it for a long time …
before letting it drop to the ground.
What is he thinking?
You notice his lips are moving … can you catch his words?
Scripture says … he mumbles.

But the words are whipped away by the wind,
which stirs up menacingly now.
Then, looking out at the towns and cities in the distance,
Jesus stands.

See how he wobbles slightly … and tries to steady himself.
But there is nothing to hold on to,
and no one to help him.
Only the enemy who pretends to be a friend …

Just imagine how it would feel, his false friend is saying now
if everyone adored and worshipped you!
I can do that for you if only …
But the *if only* is too much, and Jesus turns his back.
Scripture says … he answers …
Worship the Lord your God and serve only him.

The wind is howling now.
And as Jesus stands against the gale
his hair and clothes flap wildly.
He glances down at the rocks below as he teeters on the cliff edge.
A loose stone dislodges at his feet, and falls –
smack, smack, smacking on its journey down to the dusty ground.
What if you were to jump? the voice taunts.
You won't break, surely. Not if you are really God's son.
After a painful pause …
Jesus answers,
Do not put the Lord your God to a foolish test,
Scripture says …

And then the air is still …
The evening falls silent
and the wind rests.
Jesus too.

When you are ready bring your mind back to the classroom and open your eyes.

Reflection

- Do you think Jesus could see his enemy? How else might the devil have made his presence known?
- Why would the devil pretend to be a friend?

Why do you think Jesus quoted scripture? How might this have helped him?

How does it make us feel when we give in to temptation?

- What kinds of things tempt us?
- Pupils share with a partner about an occasion when they felt tempted. Did they manage to resist?

- What can help us to resist when we feel tempted?
- Can using words help?
- What else?

How might we help others to resist temptation?

Activities

Some suggestions …

- *Can the pupils give an example of where temptation may lead into something that is harmful? Pupils may have covered issues such as the abuse of drugs, alcohol and smoking in PSHE. In pairs, can they think of a slogan which may help someone resist if tempted?*

  Extend the above to produce a flyer warning against the dangers of giving in to this particular temptation.

- *In small groups, role play someone being tempted into something harmful to demonstrate how persuasive temptation can be. Alternatively make a Conscience Alley for a pupil to walk through. Divide the class into two lines, like an alley. One side will whisper persuasive advice giving one point of view, and the other side will offer the opposite point of view. What do the voices of temptation say? Will the pupil manage to resist? Afterwards ask the pupil what decision they made and why.*

Rule Breaker   Level 4/5

Background

1. Scripture says the Sabbath is to be kept holy (Exodus 19:8–11).
2. Pharisees were very devout. They wanted to please God and believed the way to do this was by keeping "His Law". The Law refers to the collective teachings and commands found in the first five books of Jewish scripture (*Torah*).
3. The Law contains rules about what is allowed and forbidden on the Sabbath. The Pharisees adhered strictly to these laws without exception. By healing the boy, technically Jesus was "working" and breaking the Sabbath law.
4. Jesus knew that many of the Pharisees and other Jewish officials were unhappy with his teaching and saw him as a threat to their power and influence over other Jews.

Read the New Testament account below, or tell the story in your own words.

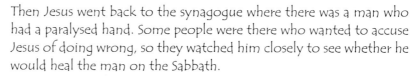

Then Jesus went back to the synagogue where there was a man who had a paralysed hand. Some people were there who wanted to accuse Jesus of doing wrong, so they watched him closely to see whether he would heal the man on the Sabbath.
Jesus said to the man,
"Come up here to the front."
Then he said to the man,
"Stretch out your hand."
He stretched it out and it became well again.

Mark 3:1–3, 5b

➤ Are there any questions or comments?

Visualisation

Sit alert and relaxed with your hands placed gently on your knees. Close your eyes, and imagine …

You are sitting in that synagogue now.

Can you feel the hardness of the cold seat through your clothing?

The place is packed and buzzing with the sound of lively hubbub.

There are many people present who don't like Jesus.

You know this because you can hear unfriendly murmurings around you.

Suddenly, the synagogue falls silent.

You watch as Jesus stands … looks at the congregation … and speaks clearly:

Is it lawful to do good on the Sabbath, or to do harm?

To save a life, or to kill?

He is looking directly at the Pharisees as he speaks, addressing this question to them.

You glance around, wondering what answer they will give …

Each one of them remains silent …

You look again at Jesus.

You can tell from his face that he is angry.

But, there's something else there too.

It's almost as though he's saddened by their silence.

You want them to answer,

but they don't.

Why won't they speak, you wonder? …

When you are ready, bring your mind back to the classroom and open your eyes.

Reflection

Do you think Jesus was right to heal on the Sabbath? Explain your answer.

- Who might want to accuse Jesus of doing wrong, and why?
- Why would this make Jesus angry?

Why might this also have made Jesus feel sad?

- Jewish scripture says it is important to keep the Sabbath day holy. Why would "work" be forbidden on the Sabbath day?
- How might the commandment to rest for one day a week be a good thing?

- Why do we have laws?
- Is there any point to having laws if we don't keep them?
- Is it always wrong to break a law?

Can you think of an occasion when it could be right to break a law?

Activities

Some suggestions …

- *Role play in groups of three or four. A follower of Jesus teams up with Pharisees outside the synagogue and tries to persuade them that Jesus is in fact living out God's Law, not breaking it. Can pupils show an understanding of both sides of the argument?*

- *Working in pairs, pupils prepare a news bulletin reporting on this controversial event in the synagogue. Ask the pupils to include quotes both for and against Jesus, to demonstrate an understanding of both sides of the argument.*

Perform or share work with the rest of the class.

Hosanna!   Level 4

Source: The New Testament: Matthew 21:1–3, 6–11 – the journey into Jerusalem.

AT1 Learning about religion: Pupils can compare public reaction to Jesus. They know that although Jesus was cheered on his journey into Jerusalem, the crowd later turned against him. They are able to suggest reasons why this might have been.

AT2 Learning from religion: Pupils can describe how being popular involves risk because people's opinions can quickly change. Pupils show understanding of how to build self-belief in others by encouraging one another with positive comments.

Vocabulary: messiah, uproar, self-belief.

Background

1. Bethphage is about 2 miles from Jerusalem.
2. The Jewish people thought of King David as the greatest king. They resented being under Roman rule, and longed for a strong leader like King David to re-emerge. They constantly lived in hope of a *messiah* who would free them from Roman government and restore the independence of Israel. *Hosanna* means "rescue us".
3. The journey into Jerusalem was the first in a series of events that led to Jesus' arrest, trial before Pilate and crucifixion. Ensure the pupils are familiar with these events, in particular the trial of Jesus (see Matthew 27:11–26). The crowd are cheering Jesus as he travels into Jerusalem, but later when Pilate asks the crowd which prisoner he should release, the people choose Barabbas over Jesus. Emphasise that initially the popular vote was with Jesus, but later the crowd turned against him.

Read the New Testament account below, or tell the story in your own words.

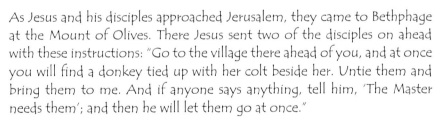

As Jesus and his disciples approached Jerusalem, they came to Bethphage at the Mount of Olives. There Jesus sent two of the disciples on ahead with these instructions: "Go to the village there ahead of you, and at once you will find a donkey tied up with her colt beside her. Untie them and bring them to me. And if anyone says anything, tell him, 'The Master needs them'; and then he will let them go at once."

So the disciples went and did what Jesus had told them to do; they brought the donkey and the colt, threw their cloaks over them, and Jesus got on. A large crowd of people spread their cloaks on the road while others cut branches from the trees and spread them on the road. The crowds walking in front of Jesus and those walking behind began to shout, "Hosanna! Praise to David's Son! God bless him who comes in the name of the Lord! Praise God!"

When Jesus entered Jerusalem, the whole city was thrown into an uproar.

"Who is he?" the people asked.

"This is the prophet Jesus from Nazareth in Galilee," the crowds answered.

Matthew 21:1–3, 6–11

➤ Are there any questions or comments?

➤ Was Jesus actually King David's son? Then why do you think the crowd call him Son of David? What do they mean?

Visualisation

Sit alert and relaxed with your hands placed gently on your knees. Close your eyes, and imagine …

It is a hot dry day.
You are walking alone on a dusty road.
Ahead you see a gathering of people …
You hear the sound of excited chatter, and wonder what is causing such interest.

As you approach the crowd you notice children carrying large branches collected from nearby trees.
The palm leaves make a green carpet as they are laid on the ground.
"HOSANNA!" they cry.

Why? You wonder …

Somebody brushes against you accidentally.
The crowd is closing in now, and you are caught up in the crush.
It is a girl, a similar age to yourself.
She apologises and giggles. You notice that her eyes are alive with expectation.
It won't be long now, she says.

What? You wonder …

Then the cheers begin. A roar of celebration almost lifts you off your feet.
People are pushing and jostling … you are losing your place.
Women are reaching forward.
Men are taking off their cloaks and throwing them on the ground …

And then you see him …
Just a glint of sun on his hair at first.
He is riding a donkey, laughing with the crowd … gently, affectionately …
touched by their adoration.

Yes, everybody loves him. All eyes are upon him …
And yet, by some strange accident,
a swift scan of the crowd, a chink in the wall of heads and shoulders,
and he finds you …

For an instant he fixes your gaze …

In his eyes you see joy,
and peace,
and strength,
and pain,
and something else you don't quite understand …

Then the moment has passed.
Somebody else pushes forward and he is lost from your vision.
You stand still for a long time, oblivious to the sights and sounds around you.

Who? You wonder …

When you are ready, bring your mind back to the classroom and open your eyes.

Reflection

Can being popular involve risk? How?

- What was it about Jesus that made him popular?
- How might people have described him?
- How do you think Jesus was feeling as he rode into Jerusalem?

The crowd seem to love Jesus now but will it last?

- What happens when Jesus arrives in Jerusalem? Does the crowd change? How?
- Can choosing to do the right thing cause a person to become unpopular?

- Do we need to be liked by others in order to like ourselves?
- Complete the following:
  I like myself because …
  I dislike myself because …
  Share with a partner.
- Can the things we say or do affect another person's self-belief? How?

How can we help to build each other's self belief?

Activities

Some suggestions …

- *Make self-belief cards. Each pupil writes their name on a card which is then passed around the class/group. On receiving a card each pupil writes a positive comment about the person named. The cards are eventually returned to their owners full of kind words that help build self-belief! Pupils can keep and read them often.*

- *Each pupil draws round one of their hands and writes their name inside the palm. Sitting in groups of five they pass their hands round, and each member of the group (including the owner of the hand) writes a positive comment in one of the fingers.*

Both the above activities give opportunity for pupils to really enjoy helping one other feel good about themselves. They can produce some amusing and sometimes surprising results!

In the Garden   Level 4

Source: The New Testament: Mark 14:32–42 – Jesus prays before his arrest.

AT1 Learning about religion: Pupils can describe what happened in the Garden of Gethsemene, and reflect on the possible feelings of Jesus at the time.

AT2 Learning from religion: Pupils share their own experiences of feeling fearful, and suggest ways of dealing with anxiety. They can consider what they might have learned from this experience.

Vocabulary: distress, anguish

Background

1. Do the pupils know what is meant by "disciple"? It means to be a follower of Jesus.
2. Explain that Jesus shared a Passover meal with his disciples shortly before his arrest, and that this was his "last supper" with them. Remind the pupils of this event by reading the New Testament account below before doing the visualisation.
3. Jesus visits the Garden of Gethsemene at night time, following the Passover meal in Jerusalem. The Garden is outside the city in a quiet place with olive trees.

Read the New Testament account below, or tell the story in your own words.

Then Jesus sent two disciples with these instructions: "Go into the city, and a man carrying a jar of water will meet you. Follow him to the house he enters and say to the owner of the house: 'The teacher says, where is the room where my disciples and I will eat the Passover meal?' Then he will show you a large upstairs room, prepared and furnished, where you will get everything ready for us."

The disciples left, went to the city, and found everything just as Jesus had told them; and they prepared the Passover meal.

When it was evening, Jesus came with the twelve disciples. While they were at the table eating, Jesus said, "I tell you that one of you will betray me – one of you that is eating with me."

The disciples were upset and began to ask him, one after the other, "Surely you don't mean me, do you?"

Mark 14:13–19

I want you to imagine you are a servant who has waited on Jesus and the disciples at the Passover meal. Because you want to know more about this man you decide to follow at a close distance when they leave the upper room. *So let's sit comfortably, alert and relaxed ... Close your eyes ... and imagine ...*

Visualisation

Something's not right.

There was a strange atmosphere in that stuffy upper room, and you want to know what's going on …

As you follow Jesus and his men through the busy streets you hear laughter and singing as others continue their Passover celebrations …

After a while, one of the disciples leaves the group and heads off up a narrow side street. Maybe he has arranged to meet other friends? …

As for you … *you* keep an eye on Jesus. You don't want to lose him …

He leads his men out of the city away from the crowds.

Up a hill where olive trees grow … to a quiet garden.

You slip in and hide behind a tree.

Can you smell the peppery scent of olives on the warm night air?

Once inside the garden the men sit down.

Although it's growing dark you can still make out their faces …

Peter … James … John …

Stay here and keep watch, you hear Jesus say to them.

But it is late, and they are tired.

They cannot keep their eyes open …

Jesus has moved further away, to be alone.

You creep forward edging between the trees, careful not to make a sound.

Peeping through the leaves you spot him,

on his knees with his face in his hands.

He is mumbling … hot, urgent whispers,

and you notice that his shoulders are shaking.

Then he crosses his arms in a tight embrace, digging his fingers into flesh.

He is like a man wrestling with himself.

Suddenly he lifts his head towards the dark sky.

He looks as though he is in pain, and you notice that his face is shining wet.

What can it be?

Tears? … Sweat? … Blood? …

Father, all things are possible for you.

Take this cup of suffering away from me!

You hear these words clearly because he almost shouts them at the sky.

Then he falls to the ground, exhausted.

With a final effort, he lifts his face.

His lips, covered with dust, begin to move in a quiet whisper.

Yet not what I want, but what you want.

You feel as though you are intruding on something very private.

A moment later Jesus is on his feet again.

You watch as he returns to find the others sleeping.

Once again, you hear his voice.

Weren't you able to stay awake, even for an hour?

Peter … James … John …

When you are ready, bring your mind back to the classroom, and open your eyes.

Reflection

- Why do you think Jesus chose to go to the Garden of Gethsemene on the Mount of Olives?
- Why might he have wanted to pray?
- The New Testament says *distress and anguish* came over Jesus in the Garden of Gethsemene. Why do you think Jesus is suffering so much?

How do you think he felt when he found his closest disciples asleep?

Can prayer help people who are feeling fearful? How?

- Although eleven disciples were present, Jesus singles out Peter, James and John. Why might this be?
- When was the last time you felt afraid? Did you talk to anyone about it, or keep it to yourself?
- Did anything else help?

- Can you think of a difficult time in your life when you needed your friends around you?
- How did your friends support you at this time?

Did anything else help?

Activities

Some suggestions …

- *List words and phrases that may describe the way Jesus was feeling that night. Write a diary-style account of events from his viewpoint.*

- *Read a sample letter from the help pages in a children's magazine. Working in pairs pupils write a letter about a worry. Each then writes a reply to the other.*

Allow opportunity for pupils to share their work.

The Arrest   Level 4

Source: The New Testament: Mark 14:41–52 – the arrest of Jesus.

AT1 *Learning about religion*: Pupils can describe what happened to Jesus at the time of his arrest and suggest reasons for his apparent passive response.

AT2 *Learning from religion*: Pupils can reflect upon their own experience of betrayal, and consider how and why they happened.

Vocabulary: earnestly, traitor, betrayal, commotion.

Background

1. This lesson should follow on from the In the Garden lesson. Recap the story so far: *Jesus prayed earnestly and urged his disciples to stay awake with him through the long night*. Explain that you will continue the story from this point, reading from the account given in the book of Mark in the New Testament.
2. Jesus knew the Jewish leaders wanted rid of him. They didn't like his behaviour in the temple when he overturned market stalls. Jesus was angry because a place of prayer had been turned into a "den of thieves" (a visualisation entitled Overturning the Temple Tables can be found in *Teaching About Jesus: practical approaches for 7–11 year olds*, p.30, RMEP, 2001). Neither did they like the fact that he seemed to have a casual approach to observing the law. The fact that Jesus was becoming very popular was also seen as a threat to their authority.
3. Check the pupils know what is meant by *torches*, *traitor* and *betraying*.
4. Explain that Judas is one of the twelve disciples, and had been a friend and follower of Jesus for a long time.

Read the New Testament account below, or tell the story in your own words.

> When he came back the third time, Jesus said to the disciples "Are you still sleeping and resting? Enough! The hour has come! Look, the Son of Man is now being handed over to the power of sinners. Get up, let us go. Look, here is the man who is betraying me."
>
> Jesus was still speaking when Judas, one of the twelve disciples, arrived. With him was a crowd armed with swords and clubs, and sent by the chief priests, the teachers of the law, and the elders. The traitor had given the crowd a signal: "The man I kiss is the one you want. Arrest him and take him away under guard."
>
> *Mark 14:41–44*

We will now imagine that we are someone who has followed Jesus and his disciples from Jerusalem up to the Garden of Gethsemene on the Mount of Olives. Judas has just arrived on the scene with a crowd of Roman soldiers. Now we're going to see what happens. *So let's sit alert and relaxed … with our hands placed gently on our knees. Close your eyes … and imagine …*

Visualisation

You are hiding behind an olive tree in the Garden of Gethsemene …
Although it's dark, you can just make out what's happening …
As you watch, you hear a commotion.
There's a crowd of people coming …
Through the trees you see the movement of flickering flames.
Can you smell the burning of torches in the night air? …
Can you hear the crowd getting louder? …
Listen. With their footsteps there is a dull sound of clanking metal.
Could they be carrying weapons? …
You crouch low, careful not to be seen.

As the crowd comes into view, you see that a number of them are carrying torches.
In the dim light you recognise that they are being led by Judas. The High Priest's slave is
there also, and some of the guards you have seen at the Temple gates.
You watch as Judas walks right up to Jesus, his little army behind him.
Will he help … or harm Jesus, do you think? …
A word is spoken. You strain to catch it …
"Teacher," says Judas, as he leans forward to kiss Jesus on the cheek.
A kiss is the greeting of a friend …

Or is it? For look what's happening now …
No sooner has he done this than the ugly crowd surrounds Jesus.
They are moving in on him, with threatening faces.
How will Jesus react? …
Will he fight them … or will he run away?

Jesus doesn't move.
But suddenly, one of his friends leaps into action.
Quickly drawing a sword he swipes at the High Priest's slave, cutting off his ear!

There's a sudden hush.
Jesus says, "Why didn't you arrest me earlier when you had the chance?"
They don't reply.
I wonder why …
As they lead Jesus away, Peter follows at a distance … the others flee.

When you are ready, bring your mind back to the classroom and open your eyes.

Reflection

- Does anything surprise or puzzle you about this account?
- Jesus didn't fight back. Nor did he run away. Why not?
- Was he being weak or strong? Explain your opinion.

Why do you think Judas betrayed Jesus?
How do you think Judas felt afterwards?

Can you think of a time when people have misunderstood your actions?

- How do you think Jesus felt when he was betrayed?
- How might the disciples have felt when Jesus was arrested?

- Have you ever felt let down by a friend?
- How did it make you feel?

Can you think of a time when you let someone down who trusted you?

Activities

Some suggestions …

- *Write a letter of apology or explanation from Judas to Jesus.*

- *Write a letter of apology or explanation to the person you let down.*

- *Paint a picture entitled "Betrayal".*

Create opportunity for pupils to share and talk about their work.

Dead or Alive?　　　Level 4

> **Source**: The New Testament: Luke 24:1–12 – the women's resurrection account.
>
> **AT1 Learning about religion**: Pupils are familiar with Luke's version of events surrounding the resurrection story. They know that for Christians this is the most important of all the stories about Jesus, and can accept that this story is full of mystery. They raise questions that are unanswerable, and refer to the beliefs of others.
>
> **AT2 Learning from religion**: Pupils can reflect on whether it is possible to believe things that seem to contradict reason.
>
> **Vocabulary**: Resurrection, crucifixion.

Background

> 1. The Sabbath (beginning at dusk on Friday evening) was a day of rest for Jewish people when no work was allowed.
> 2. Jesus was crucified on Friday so nothing could be done to give him a proper burial until the first day of the week (Sunday).
> 3. In Israel, tombs were often carved out of rock faces or caves. The body would have been wrapped in long linen strips soaked with sweet smelling spices (anointing). The body could then be laid on a slab of rock.
> 4. Usually the tomb was closed by rolling a huge circular stone in front of the entrance.

Read the New Testament account below, or tell the story in your own words.

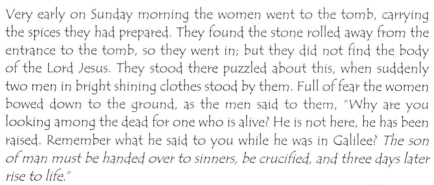

Very early on Sunday morning the women went to the tomb, carrying the spices they had prepared. They found the stone rolled away from the entrance to the tomb, so they went in; but they did not find the body of the Lord Jesus. They stood there puzzled about this, when suddenly two men in bright shining clothes stood by them. Full of fear the women bowed down to the ground, as the men said to them, "Why are you looking among the dead for one who is alive? He is not here, he has been raised. Remember what he said to you while he was in Galilee? *The son of man must be handed over to sinners, be crucified, and three days later rise to life.*"

Luke 24:1–7

> ➤ Are there any questions or comments?
> ➤ What do you think happened next?
> ➤ Explain that the women then went to find the disciples to share the news. In the visualisation we will "tag along" with them to see for ourselves the reaction of the disciples.
> ➤ Remind the pupils that Peter was the disciple who denied knowing Jesus after his arrest, and later "wept bitterly" (Luke 22:62).

Visualisation

Sit alert and relaxed with your hands placed gently on your knees. Close your eyes, and imagine ...

You'll never believe it! ... one of the women cries,
as they burst through the door.
You slip in behind them to share the exciting news.

Inside the room, the disciples are huddled together,
looking all lost and forlorn,
wondering what to do with themselves
now it's all over,
and he is gone.

How will they react to this wonderful news? ...

You quickly scan their faces ...
What do you find there? Is it what you expect?
Shock? ... surprise? ... confusion? ... .mistrust?

There is silence for a moment.
And then in turn they speak.

You must be mad!
You must be dreaming!
It can't be true, we all saw him crucified!

Again, in turn each woman tells her tale
exactly as she saw it for herself ...
Then, in their eagerness, all talk at once,
finishing each other's sentences.
Such is their desire to be heard
and believed.

Yet disbelief is written all over each disciple's face.
You'll never believe it! ... was never more true.
For all except one.
One man's face melts into something new ...
Take a close look now at Peter,
as the sun streams in through the open window.
What do you see behind his eyes?

Hope? ... Fear? ... Wonder?
The moment is gone, for he rushes past you, muttering something under his breath
as he heads for the door.
Did you catch what he said? ...

The others look at one another with puzzled faces.
You'll never believe it! ...
  ... Will you?

When you are ready, bring your mind back to the classroom and open your eyes.

Reflection

Is something true only if it can be explained?

- Where did Peter go, and why would he be in such a rush to get there?
- What might Peter have said as he left the room?

Do we have to see something for ourselves to believe it happened?

- Why did the disciples disbelieve the women?
- How do you think this made the women feel?

- What explanation did the men in shining clothes give?
- Why do you think their explanation convinced the women but not the disciples?
- If something cannot be explained, does this make it "untrue"? Why? Why not?

How might belief in the resurrection affect the life of a Christian?

Activities

Some suggestions …

- *In groups pupils freeze frame …*

  – the women entering the room
  – the reaction of the disciples.

  Invite each group to show their freeze frame to the class and discuss interpretations.

  (Freeze frames could be photographed for display alongside quotes of the pupil's explanations).

- *Pupils imagine they are Peter. Think about what he found when he arrived at the tomb, and what questions he would like answering. Either …*

  – Write a journal entry OR
  – Write a letter to a friend explaining what you found.

Stories Jesus told

The Lost Coin

Source: The New Testament: Luke 15:8–10 – the Parable of the Lost Coin.

AT1 Learning about Religion: Pupils can describe the parable of the Lost Coin and its meaning. They ask questions about religious terminology.

AT2 Learning from Religion: Pupils can think about things that are valuable to them, in particular things that are not easily replaced if lost. They compare notions of material and sentimental value.

Vocabulary: Pharisee, outcast, repent, sinner, parable.

Religious vocabulary: Pharisee, outcast, repent, sinner.

Background

1. Explain that a parable is a story with another meaning. Jesus often used parables to teach people about God.
2. Tax collectors were usually Jews employed by the Romans to collect taxes during New Testament times. They were allowed to keep a "fraction" for themselves, but because there was no law controlling the rates they charged, tax collectors were often greedy, taking more than a fair share. Because of this they were disliked and often seen as traitors among their own people.
3. What do the pupils understand "outcast" to mean? According to Jewish Law those who were "unclean" must be isolated from the rest of the community (even literally cast outside the city walls) until such time as the priest declared them ritually clean once again. The cause of uncleanness may have been leprosy, or certain other bodily conditions. A person could also become ritually unclean by contact with a dead body or by eating certain animals. The laws surrounding ritual cleanliness are found in the book of Leviticus.
4. The Pharisees were Jewish teachers of the (religious) Law.

Read the New Testament account below, or tell the story in your own words.

One day, when many tax collectors and other outcasts came to listen to Jesus, the Pharisees and teachers of the Law started grumbling, "This man welcomes outcasts and even eats with them!" So Jesus told them this parable …

"Suppose a woman who has ten silver coins loses one of them – what does she do?

She lights a lamp, sweeps her house, and looks carefully everywhere until she finds it.

When she finds it, she calls her friends and neighbours together, and says to them,

"I am so happy I found the coin I lost. Let us celebrate!"

In the same way I tell you the angels of God rejoice over one sinner who repents."

Luke 15:1–3,8–10

- Are there any questions or comments?
- What is the parable about?
- Could the parable have any other meaning?
- What point might Jesus want to make in telling this story to the Pharisees?

Visualisation

Sit alert and relaxed with your hands placed gently on your knees. Close your eyes and imagine …

You are standing in front of a raised glass cube.
It is similar to a display cabinet you would see in a jeweller's shop, or a museum …
But much bigger.
In fact it is a chamber almost as large as the classroom.
It is called the Chamber of Safekeeping.
If you want to, walk round it and look at all the things inside …

You will notice that there are lots of things inside the glass chamber.
These things have been placed there for safe-keeping.
They are things that are precious to people.
Things they don't want to lose.

Look closely, and try to remember what you see …

As you walk around the outside of the glass chamber you notice some steps leading to a door at one corner.
The door has been opened, and you are invited to enter …
Now you can take an even closer look,
and perhaps touch some of the things you see …

Something shiny catches your eye, and you bend to pick it up.
It is a silver coin. Can you feel its heavy cool weight on your open palm?
As you turn it over you realise it is the very coin that was lost.
The coin in the story, that was very precious to the woman,
So much so, she searched high and low all day until she found it.
Once found, she must have placed it inside this Chamber of Safekeeping.
Now it will never be lost again.

As you glance around the glass chamber you notice an empty space.
It has been reserved for you …
Can you think of something you might want to place there? …
Something that is precious to you? …
Something you want to keep safe? …
Something you would be sad to lose? …

Perhaps more than one thing comes to mind? …
In your imagination see yourself placing your treasure in that little space
Where you know it will remain …
Inside the glass Chamber of Safekeeping
Forevermore …

When you are ready, bring your mind back to the classroom, and open your eyes.

Reflection

List some of the things that have sentimental value.

- Ask the children what kind of things they saw inside the Chamber of Safekeeping.
- Were all these things "precious" in the same way?

List some of the things that have material or monetary value.

- Can things be precious to one person but not to another?
- Some things are not easily replaced once lost. What kind of things?
- What makes these things precious?

- Invite the children to talk about some of the things they placed within the Chamber of Safekeeping during the visualisation.

Can the pupils explain their choices?

Activities

Some suggestions …

- *Pupils draw a precious item around which they write words describing its meaning for them.*

- *Teacher makes a large cube template from paper (2D image). Pupils each draw a precious item. Pupils then take turns coming forward to place their item "inside" the cube.*

The Reckless Son Level 4/5

Source: The New Testament: Luke 15:11–32 – the Parable of the Prodigal Son.

AT1 Learning about religion: Pupils can explain that parables are stories with another meaning. They are able to reflect upon the implicit meaning of the parable of the Prodigal Son.

AT2 Learning from religion: Pupils consider the idea that parental love can be unconditional and go beyond usual expectations of fairness. They suggest how unconditional love might influence people.

Vocabulary: reckless, famine, inherit, inheritance, unconditional.

Background

1. This story is traditionally known as the Parable of the Prodigal Son.
2. Explain that Jewish law prohibits the eating of pork because the pig is regarded as "unclean". This shows the depths to which this Jewish son sank by living among the pigs and eating their swill.
3. Hired workers were not regular employees, but were simply hired by the day. Their welfare was therefore uncertain; they could be out of work and penniless the following day.

Read the New Testament account below, or tell the story in your own words.

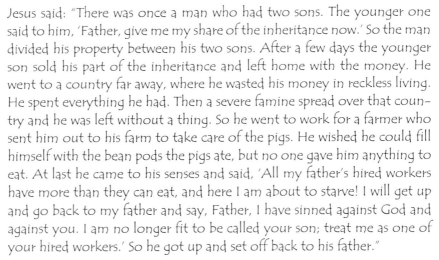

Jesus said: "There was once a man who had two sons. The younger one said to him, 'Father, give me my share of the inheritance now.' So the man divided his property between his two sons. After a few days the younger son sold his part of the inheritance and left home with the money. He went to a country far away, where he wasted his money in reckless living. He spent everything he had. Then a severe famine spread over that country and he was left without a thing. So he went to work for a farmer who sent him out to his farm to take care of the pigs. He wished he could fill himself with the bean pods the pigs ate, but no one gave him anything to eat. At last he came to his senses and said, 'All my father's hired workers have more than they can eat, and here I am about to starve! I will get up and go back to my father and say, Father, I have sinned against God and against you. I am no longer fit to be called your son; treat me as one of your hired workers.' So he got up and set off back to his father."

Luke 15:11–20

➤ What do you suppose will happen when the reckless son returns to his father?
➤ Do you think he is making a mistake?
➤ How do you think the father will react?

Let's join the story at this point. I want you to imagine that *you* are the reckless son. You have frittered away all the money your father gave you and now you have nothing left. You have decided to travel home, to confess everything to your father, and to say sorry …

Visualisation

Sit alert and relaxed with your hands placed gently on your knees. Close your eyes, and imagine …

Your feet are sore … your throat is dry … and your empty stomach aches …
Worst of all, your heart is heavy as you tread the long road home.
Heavy as you think of all that has been lost and wasted …
In the pit of your stomach there's a sick, sad feeling, as you wonder …
What will your father say? …

As you approach the familiar building you see hired workers in the fields.
You notice they look strong and well.
And you envy them, for in truth, their life is so much better than yours right now.
How you wish, like them, you could drink clean water, and maybe eat some of the bruised
fruit that has fallen to the ground …

What will your father say? …
"It serves you right," probably.
Why should he give you work? Why a second chance? …
No doubt he will be angry and send you packing for making a dreadful mess of everything,
and being such a disappointment to him …

And then there's your elder brother. What will *he* say! …
The sensible one, who stayed and worked hard,
saving his money for the future – for his children's wellbeing …
Only he is fit to be called a son.
Not you.

You are just about to lose your nerve and turn back
when you catch something in the air … the delicious smell of roasting meat.
It pins you to the spot.
You hear music too … and dancing … and joyful laughter in the distance …
It is painful to your ears … this sound of other people's happiness.

And then you hear the unmistakable voice of your father.
You see him running towards you. He speaks just two words:
"My son!" …
Before you have a chance to reply, a rich cloak is thrown over your shoulders, and you are
bustled inside where tables are heavy with food and drink,
into the warmth of a welcome party …
"I saw you approaching from far away," he is saying now, excitedly.
"I thought you were lost. This calls for a celebration!"

"But … " You cannot speak. You do not understand.
Maybe he doesn't know what has happened … doesn't fully realise what you have done.
But when you look into his eyes you see that indeed your father knows everything.
Everything!
Yet still his arms are open wide …
Welcoming you home …

When you are ready, bring your mind back to the classroom and open your eyes.

Reflection

Is the love of a parent unconditional?

- Did anything in the visualisation surprise you?
- What might the reckless son have been feeling as he approached home?
- How might the older son have felt; both towards his brother and towards his father?

Is the father's behaviour fair? Explain.

- Does the reckless son deserve to be forgiven?
- Not only does the father forgive his son, he celebrates his return with a lavish party! Why would he do this?
- How would the father's welcome make the reckless son feel?

- Jesus used parables to teach about God.
- When Jesus told this story he didn't explain its other meaning. Have you any ideas about what this might be?

What might this parable say about what God is like?

Activities

Some suggestions ...

- *The visualisation covers only part of the parable – the older son's reaction is missing. Read Luke 15:25–32 and invite the pupils to act out the scene and perform in groups to the class.*

- *The strong emotions felt by both sons lend themselves to role play. The older son may vent anger about the unfairness of it all; the younger son may feel a mixture of guilt and gratitude. Teacher-led hot-seating will provide opportunity to unravel and discuss these feelings. The father could also be hot-seated to reveal his motives.*

Prejudice Level 4/5

> **Source:** The New Testament: Luke 10:25–37 – the Parable of the Good Samaritan.
>
> **AT1 Learning about religion:** Pupils can describe how in the parable of the Good Samaritan Jesus condemned racial prejudice, and taught people to love their neighbour. They can explain how Jesus valued kindness to others above strict observance of religious law.
>
> **AT2 Learning from religion:** The pupils are able to imagine a situation in which they might have feelings of prejudice. They can reflect upon what influences these feelings and consider how to deal with them.
>
> **Vocabulary:** Samaritan, Levite.

Background

1. Jesus had been talking with a teacher of the Law. They were discussing the importance of the *Golden Rule* which sums up the teaching of scripture in a nutshell: "*Love the Lord your God with all your heart, with all your soul, with all your strength, and with all your mind; and love your neighbour as you love yourself.*" The teacher of the Law then asked Jesus, "Who is my neighbour?" Jesus told the parable of the Good Samaritan in response to this question.

2. The Samaritans were a mixed-race group of people from Samaria who were neither pure Jew nor Gentile (Greek). The Jews of neighbouring Judea and Galilee disliked Samaritans because they were not true Jews. In this parable Jesus addresses issues of racial prejudice prevalent in New Testament times.

3. A Levite was someone from the tribe of Levi, with duties to serve in the Temple.

4. Priests needed to be ritually clean at all times. They certainly shouldn't touch a dead body as this would make them ritually unclean and exclude them from the Temple. This could explain why the priest walked by.

Ask the pupils to find the reference in the New Testament, read together or retell the story in your own words.

"Who is my neighbour?"

Jesus answered, "There was once a man who was going down from Jerusalem to Jericho when robbers attacked him, stripped him, and beat him up, leaving him half dead. It so happened that a priest was going down that road; but when he saw the man, he walked on by, on the other side. In the same way a Levite also came along, went over and looked at the man, and then walked on by, on the other side. But a Samaritan who was travelling that way came upon the man, and when he saw him, his heart was filled with pity. He went over to him, poured oil and wine on his wounds and bandaged them; then he put the man on his own animal and took him to an inn, where he took care of him. The next day he took out two silver coins and gave them to the inn-keeper. "Take care of him," he told the innkeeper, "and when I come back this way, I will pay you whatever else you spend on him."

And Jesus concluded, "In your opinion, which one of these three acted like a neighbour towards the man attacked by the robbers?" The teacher of the Law answered, "The one who was kind to him."

Jesus replied, "You, go then, and do the same." *Luke 10:29–37*

➤ Are there any questions or comments?

➤ Why do you think the priest and the Levite walked by without helping the man?

➤ The Samaritan showed more compassion than the priest and the Levite? I wonder why?

➤ How might any Jew have felt on hearing that a Samaritan helped the injured person?

➤ What point might Jesus have wanted to make by telling the parable?

Visualisation

Sit alert and relaxed with your hands placed gently on your knees. Close your eyes, and imagine …

You have been told that you can invite someone to your home for a sleepover.
See yourself now in your room at home, among all your familiar things.
Prepare the room for your guest …
Tidy up any mess, and make it look nice …
Clear a place for your guest to sit …
Select the games you will play … things you will look at … music you might listen to …

Now see yourself in the kitchen preparing a tray of snacks for the evening.
What food will you choose? …
What will you have to drink? …
See yourself pouring two drinks and placing them on the tray …
Add the food you have chosen …
Now you are ready for your guest to arrive.

Who will you decide to invite to your sleepover? …

Bring to mind the face of somebody you *like* …
I wonder why you chose this person? …
What is it about them you like? …
Is it the way they look? …
Is it the way they speak? …
Is it because of the things they say? …
Is it because of the things they do? …
Imagine this person sitting here in your room right now, among your things …
How does it feel to have them as your guest? …
Look them in the eye, and tell them: *I like you because* …
If you want to, offer your guest some of the food and drink you have prepared …

Now bring to mind the face of somebody you *dislike* …
I wonder why you chose this person? …
What is it about them you dislike? …
Is it the way they look? …
Is it the way they speak? …
Is it because of the things they say? …
Is it because of the things they do? …
Imagine them sitting here in your room right now, among your things …
How does it feel to have them as your guest? …
Look them in the eye and tell them: *I dislike you because* …
If you want to, offer your guest some of the food and drink you have prepared …

When you are ready, bring your mind back to the classroom and open your eyes.

Reflection

- Did anything in the visualisation surprise you?
- Did your feelings change during the visualisation?
- How?

Was there a difference in the way you treated your two guests? Explain.

Do we tend to like only people who are similar to ourselves?

- What makes us decide we like or dislike someone?
- Is this fixed, or can it change? If so, what might cause our opinions to changes?

- The *Golden Rule* Jesus referred to in the story says *"Love your neighbour as yourself"*.
- What kind of love would Jesus be talking about?
- Is it possible to love someone we dislike? How?

Who is *'your neighbour'*?

Activities

Some suggestions …

- *Dramatise the parable of the Good Samaritan.*

- *Hot seat the priest, Levite and Good Samaritan. Invite pupils to act in role as each character, taking questions from the rest of the class.*

- *Draw a comic strip portraying the parable. Use thought bubbles to indicate the motives behind the actions of the characters in the story.*

Small Beginnings   Level 4

> **Source**: The New Testament: Mark 4:30–34 – the Parable of the Mustard Seed.
>
> **AT1 Learning about religion**: Pupils know that Jesus explained about the Kingdom of God using parables. Pupils can describe the parable of the mustard seed, and show an understanding of its meaning.
>
> **AT2 Learning from religion**: Pupils can describe small beginnings in relation to their own lives. They can refer to a situation where the actions of an individual grew to something that had a big impact on the world.
>
> **Vocabulary**: parable, Kingdom of God.

This story presents a wonderful opportunity for a visual aid. Mustard seeds are commonly used in Indian and eastern recipes and can be found in most supermarkets these days. It is a nice idea for the storytelling, to place a single mustard seed in the palm of each child's hand. They will be fascinated, and the parable will have real meaning. As an additional challenge – how well can they look after their mustard seed? Perhaps offer a reward to everyone who can return their seed to you at the end of the lesson!

Background

1. Parables are stories that have more than one meaning. Jesus used parables to explain the Kingdom of God and when teaching about the big questions in life.
2. The mustard plant can grow from a tiny seed to a great height in just a few weeks. Southern species in Israel have been known to reach between 10–16 feet tall.
3. In autumn the branches become rigid and the plant serves as a shelter for birds.

Read the New Testament account below, or tell the story in your own words.

"What shall we say the Kingdom of God is like?" asked Jesus.

"What parable shall we use to explain it? It is like this. A man takes a mustard seed, the smallest seed in the world, and plants it in the ground. After a while it grows up and becomes the biggest of all plants. It puts out such large branches that the birds come and make their nests in its shade."

Mark 4:30–32

➤ Are there any questions or comments?
➤ What is this parable about?

Visualisation

Sit alert and relaxed with your hands placed gently on your knees. Close your eyes and imagine …

You hold a tiny mustard seed in the palm of your hand.
See how small it is … and dark … like a worthless speck of dirt.
The lines and folds of skin hold it in place for now …
But it could so easily fall to the ground and be lost,
If.. you are not careful …

Now imagine yourself many miles away, to the east, in the land of Israel …
Here a tiny mustard seed is planted in a field of fertile soil …
The sun warms the earth …
The farmer tends and waters it … and soon a shoot appears …
Watch as it grows…
Twisting … and turning …
Reaching up towards the light …
Its purplish-green stems spread high and wide.
And now, look …
At the end of the branches small clusters of yellow flowers appear …

Would you like to step nearer to take a closer look? …
See how many flowers make up one cluster …
And then, just think … for every flower that dies,
Ten new seeds will emerge from the pod …

There must be *hundreds* of flowers on this plant …
That means *thousands* of seeds …
Enough to plant an entire field …
All from this single plant that you have watched grow
from a tiny mustard seed …

Looking up now, at the tallest branches, you reach high above your head …
Can you feel yourself wobble as you stretch on tiptoes? …
Even when you try to jump
You still cannot reach the highest leaf …

Now it's time to leave the field of the mustard plant.
You turn to walk away.
And open your palm to look once again at the tiny seed you hold there …

Then, for a last time, you turn and look at the field …
You see a magnificent sunshine yellow blanket
made up of so many flowers …
and countless small beginnings
yet to come …

When you are ready, bring your mind back to the classroom … and open your eyes.

Reflection

Did that small beginning grow? Does it continue to grow?

- Was there anything in the visualisation that surprised you?
- Jesus used the parable of the mustard seed to explain about the Kingdom of God.

What point might Jesus have wanted to make about the Kingdom of God?

- When you started school you could only just write your name. Now you can write a whole page of neatly joined writing!
- Can you think of any other small beginnings in your life?

- Can you think of a small act of kindness done by you, or done for you? Make two lists.
- Are these acts of kindness done only for people we know, or for people we don't know?

Can our small actions have a big impact on others? How?

Activities

Some suggestions …

- *Find out about an historical example of small beginnings; where the actions of one person grew into something that had a big impact on others. For example, Bob Geldoff's visit to Africa during the droughts of 1985 leading to the Live Aid concert raising £30 million.*

- *Think about some possible outcomes for the small acts of kindness that have been listed. This could be shown visually as a plant drawing where the outcomes are written inside the leaves. A large-scale version could make an attractive display!*

The Humble Man Level 4

Source: The New Testament: Luke 18:9–14 – the Parable of the Pharisee and the Tax Collector.

AT1 *Learning about religion*: Pupils can recount the parable of the Pharisee and the tax collector and have some understanding of their respective roles in New Testament times. They can discern the difference in motives between the Pharisee and the tax collector.

AT2 *Learning from religion*: Pupils understand the meaning of "self-righteous" and "judgemental" and can describe examples of behaviour that show these attitudes.

Vocabulary: humble, boast, self-righteous, judgemental, despised, tephillin.

Background

1. Pharisees were religious teachers who were very strict about keeping the Law exactly as written in scripture. A Pharisee would wear a tephillin, a small box strapped to the forehead containing words from the Torah (Hebrew law – see Deuteronomy 6:4–9).
2. Though there were many possible days of fasting in the Jewish calendar, Jews were only required to fast on one day of the year – the Day of the Atonement.
3. Tax collectors were usually Jews employed by the Romans to collect taxes during New Testament times. They were allowed to keep a "fraction" for themselves, but because there was no law controlling the rates they charged, tax collectors were often greedy, taking more than a fair share. Because of this they were disliked, and often seen as traitors among their own people.
4. The Temple was in Jerusalem. It had several courtyards; the outer one being the only place that Gentiles (non-Jews) were allowed to enter and pray.
5. Tithing is the Jewish practice of giving one tenth of one's income to the work of God.

The pupils do not need to be told the story before doing the visualisation. The New Testament account below is for the teacher's reference only.

Jesus told this parable to people who were sure of their own goodness and despised everybody else:

Once there were two men who went up to the Temple to pray. One was a Pharisee, the other a tax collector. The Pharisee stood apart by himself and prayed, "I thank you God that I am not greedy, I am not dishonest and I do not commit adultery like everybody else. I thank you that I am not like that tax collector over there. I fast two days a week, and I give you a tenth of all my income."

The tax collector stood at a distance and would not even raise his face to heaven, but beat his chest and said, "God have pity on me, a sinner!"

"I tell you," said Jesus, "the tax collector and not the Pharisee was in the right with God when he went home. For all who make themselves great will be humbled, and all who humble themselves will be made great."

Luke 18:9–14

Visualisation

Sit alert and relaxed with your hands placed gently on your knees. Close your eyes, and imagine …

You are a little bird perching high on the Temple wall in Jerusalem.
From here you can see all the comings and goings as people pass
in and out of the Temple …
Today you see a man standing in the court of the Jews.
He wears a tephillin on his forehead –
a little box containing some very precious words of the Law.
This reminds him to keep the Law at the front of his mind … as he believes is pleasing to God.
He is a very religious man:
a Pharisee.

You watch his mouth moving as he stands to make his prayer.
A prayer of thanksgiving for everything that is good in his life.
"I thank you God, that I have kept every part of your Law," he says in a loud voice.
"I am not greedy … I am not dishonest … and I do not cheat on my wife like so many other people do."
"I thank you that I am not like that tax collector over there," he adds
with a disapproving sideways glance.
"I fast for two days a week, and I give a tenth of all my income to you."

You watch as he lifts his smug face towards heaven …
Perhaps he is waiting for a smile from God …
or a pat on the back?
What might he be thinking, you wonder? …

Now you flutter "over there", to the other side of the courtyard.
Another man is standing with his face to the floor.
Although he is a Jew, he is not a religious man.
He is a tax collector.

You hop close to where he stands … and you notice
this man's shoulders sag with sadness.
His mouth is moving, but you cannot hear his prayer.
So you hop even closer towards him.
He is on his knees now … covering his face with his hands.
From here you hear his private whispers.
"Oh God, I have failed to keep your Law.
Have mercy on me, a sinner."
What might he be thinking, you wonder? …

He stays there for a while.
Long after the Pharisee has left.
You want to stay too, but the footsteps of new arrivals make you afraid.
You fly away to the safety of the wall.
Then higher still, to the very pinnacle of the Temple,
where, from a great height,
you look down upon the humble man
and smile.

When you are ready, bring your mind back to the classroom and open your eyes.

Reflection

- The Pharisee believed that everything he did pleased God, and he boasted about always doing the right thing.
- This is an example of being *self-righteous*.

How do you feel when you *know* you are right about something? Discuss.

Do we sometimes judge other people? Discuss and give examples.

- The Pharisee complained about other people who didn't do the right thing.
- This is an example of being *judgemental*.

- How do you think the Pharisee was feeling as he prayed?
- How do you think the tax collector was feeling as he prayed?
- Whose prayer would please God most? Why?

Why do you think Jesus told this parable? What would he want people to learn from it?

Activities

Some suggestions …

- *Role play in pairs. One pupil is the tax collector, the other the Pharisee. Each explains to the other their way of praying, justifying themselves. Choose pairs to perform in front of the class. Allow time for pupils watching to comment.*

- *Give each pupil two small pieces of paper (preferably use two different shades). On one, ask them to write a sentence about something they "got right" or did well. On the other piece of paper write a sentence about something they didn't get right or do well. Invite pupils to share their responses in a circle time. After sharing, pupils could pin their responses onto a board. This would create a visual aid for the class showing a healthy balance between pride and humility. Alternatively pupils could draw rather than write their responses.*

The Sower   Level 4/5

> **Source**: The New Testament: Mark 4:1–9, 13–20 – the Parable of the Sower.
>
> **AT1 Learning about religion**: Pupils know that Jesus used parables in his teaching. They know that parables are stories with metaphorical meaning. They can suggest an interpretation of the parable of the Sower.
>
> **AT2 Learning from religion**: Pupils have some understanding of how metaphor is used in the parable of the Sower. They can talk about the parable's imagery in a way that is meaningful to them, and reflect on what conditions in life help them and others to grow as people.
>
> **Vocabulary**: parable, interpretation.

Background

> Jesus often used parables to explain about the Kingdom of God and the big questions of life. Sometimes the interpretation is left open. However the gospel accounts often record that Jesus gave a private explanation to his disciples following his public teaching. This parable is one such example. Read further along in the text from Mark 4:13–20 and decide if you want to give pupils the New Testament explanation also. If you do this, allow opportunity for pupils to give their own answers to the questions below, before giving them the traditional interpretation.

Ask the pupils to find the reference in the New Testament, read together or retell the story in your own words.

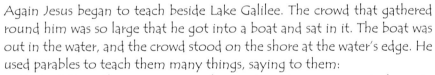

Again Jesus began to teach beside Lake Galilee. The crowd that gathered round him was so large that he got into a boat and sat in it. The boat was out in the water, and the crowd stood on the shore at the water's edge. He used parables to teach them many things, saying to them:

"Listen! Once there was a man who went out to sow corn. As he scattered the seed in the field, some of it fell along the path, where the birds came and ate it up. Some of it fell on rocky ground, where there was little soil. The seeds soon sprouted, because the soil wasn't deep. Then, when the sun came up, it burnt the young plants; and because the roots had not grown deep enough, the plants soon dried up. Some of the seed fell among thorn bushes, which grew up and choked the plants, and they didn't produce any corn. But some seeds fell in good soil, and the plants sprouted, grew, and produced corn: some had thirty grains, others sixty, and others a hundred."

Jesus concluded, "Listen, then, if you have ears!"

Mark 4:1–9

➤ Are there any questions?
➤ What might the parable be about?
➤ What could it mean?

Visualisation

Sit alert and relaxed with your hands placed gently on your knees. Close your eyes, and imagine …

Today you will explore an island.

The first place you visit is cold and windy. Ahead of you is a steep cliff face. You are completely alone …

Walking is difficult here because the ground is uneven. It is scattered with rocks that cause you to stumble. Sometimes large boulders block your way completely. Your throat is dry, your legs ache, and you feel tired with the effort of climbing …

Now imagine a seed falling upon this place. Watch as it lands. See how a bird swoops down to eat the seed …

Move on now, to another part of the island …

Picture yourself walking along a wide, open path. Here you are not alone anymore. Many other people are walking also in both directions and the air is thick with the hustle and bustle of comings and goings. The earth is very hard here because it has been well trodden.

I wonder…what would happen if the seed were to fall here? …

Leave this place now, and take yourself to a wide, open meadow. A gentle breeze touches your hair and the morning sun is warm on your face. Beneath your feet the grass is soft and springy …
Fill your lungs with the fresh, clean air. Relax and enjoy … This is a good place to be. As you stand here you feel happy and immensely thankful for all the good things in your life …

Imagine what will happen when a seed falls here? Watch and see for yourself …

Now zoom out and see the whole island from up above …
Notice that seeds are falling everywhere …
all over the island, in every place.
On rocky ground … on stony paths …and on fertile land …

The Sower scatters the seed everywhere.
Some will be lost …
Others will grow … and grow …

When you are ready, bring your mind back to the classroom and open your eyes.

Reflection

- What part of the visualisation did you enjoy?
- Did your feelings change during the visualisation? In what way?

Who might the Sower be?

What do we need to help us grow – to become the kind of people we want to be?

- Where on the island is the seed most likely to grow? Why?
- What conditions does a seed need to help it grow?

- What kinds of things prevent us from achieving this?
- What is the "hard ground" in your life – where you struggle most? Can you share this with a partner?

What is the meadowland where you find most happiness?

Activities

Some suggestions …

- *Teacher draws a map of an island on the board. Ask the pupils where they want to place different terrain conditions: rocky, mountainous, forest, town, meadowland, lakes and rivers. As a whole class, think of metaphorical names that match feelings associated with the type of terrain; for example, Fearful Forest, Struggle Mountain, Meadow of Delight.*

- *"My Island" – Pupils draw a map of an island, showing a range of different terrain conditions as relates to their own life. Encourage the pupils to write words on the drawing to make the island personal to them; for example, spelling tests or learning the 8 x table may be mountainous, listening to favourite music or time spent with friends may be meadowland.*